LET'S LEARN ABOUT...
THE SKY

PROJECT BOOK

STEAM

T0346098

K3

 Pearson

Pearson Education Limited
KAO Two, KAO Park, Harlow, Essex, CM17 9NA, England
and Associated Companies around the world

First published 2020
Second impression 2024

ISBN: 978-1-292-33452-3

Set in Mundo Sans
Printed in Slovakia by Neografia

Acknowledgements
The publishers and author(s) would like to thank the following people and institutions for their feedback and comments during the development of the material: Marcos Mendonça, Leandra Dias, Viviane Kirmeliene, Rhiannon Ball, Mônica Bicalho and GB Editorial. The publishers would also like to thank all the teachers who contributed to the development of *Let's learn about...*: Adriano de Paula Souza, Aline Ramos Teixeira Santo, Aline Vitor Rodrigues Pina Pereira, Ana Paula Gomez Montero, Anna Flávia Feitosa Passos, Camila Jarola, Celiane Junker Silva, Edegar França Junior, Fabiana Reis Yoshio, Fernanda de Souza Thomaz, Luana da Silva, Michael Iacovino Luidvinavicius, Munique Dias de Melo, Priscila Rossatti Duval Ferreira Neves, Sandra Ferito, and schools that took part in Construindo Juntos.

Author Acknowledgements
Luciana Pinheiro and Gisele Aga

Image Credit(s):
123RF.com: Mousemd 39; **Pearson Education Ltd:** 5, 7, 9, 21, 23, 25, 27, 29, 31, 33, 37, 41, 43, 47, 51, 53, 55, 57, 59, 61, 63, 65, 71, 71, Debanjan Basak 39; **Shutterstock.com:** Alan Uster 49, Brovko Serhii 69, Bus109 19, Greiss Design 45, Johavel 69, 69, Juli Hansen 39, KittyVector 19, 39, 39, 69, 69, Lynxvector 19, 19, Maike Hildebrandt 69, Mything 39, Newelle 13, 69, Pogorelova Olga 69, Psmans Xyz 69, Studio G 69, Victor Brave 11, 11, 11, 17, 17, 17, 17, 17, 69, 69, 69, 69

Illustration Acknowledgements
Illustrated by Filipe Laurentino and MRS Editorial.

Cover illustration © Filipe Laurentino

CONTENTS

U1   WHO DO YOU LIKE TO PLAY WITH?   5

U2   WHAT PARTS OF YOUR BODY HELP YOU FEEL?   13

U3   WHY IS YOUR FAMILY IMPORTANT TO YOU?   21

U4   WHAT HAPPENS TO YOUR BODY WHEN YOU
     ARE HOT OR COLD?   29

U5   WHY IS IT IMPORTANT TO TAKE CARE OF OUR PLANET?   37

U6   HOW CAN YOU STAY HEALTHY?   45

U7   HOW CAN YOU TAKE CARE OF ANIMALS?   53

U8   WHAT IS YOUR FAVORITE PLACE IN TOWN?   61

STICKERS   69

LOOK AND COLOR RAPUNZEL'S HAIR. HOW LONG IS HER HAIR? 👁 ✏

COLOR THE SHAPES. USE THEM TO BUILD YOUR OWN CASTLE.

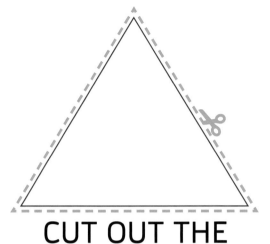

CUT OUT THE TRIANGLE ROOF.

CUT OUT THE RECTANGLE TOWER.

CUT OUT THE SQUARE CASTLE WALL.

CUT OUT THE RECTANGLE DOOR.

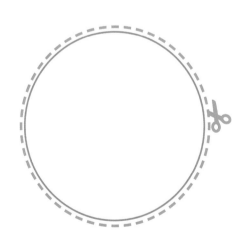

CUT OUT THE CIRCLE WINDOW.

MAKE A PATTERN FOR THE SNAKE'S SKIN.

MAKE YOUR OWN SONG USING BODY SOUNDS.

CLAP HANDS

STOMP FOOT

SNAP FINGERS

_____

_____

_____

_____

LOOK AND DRAW.

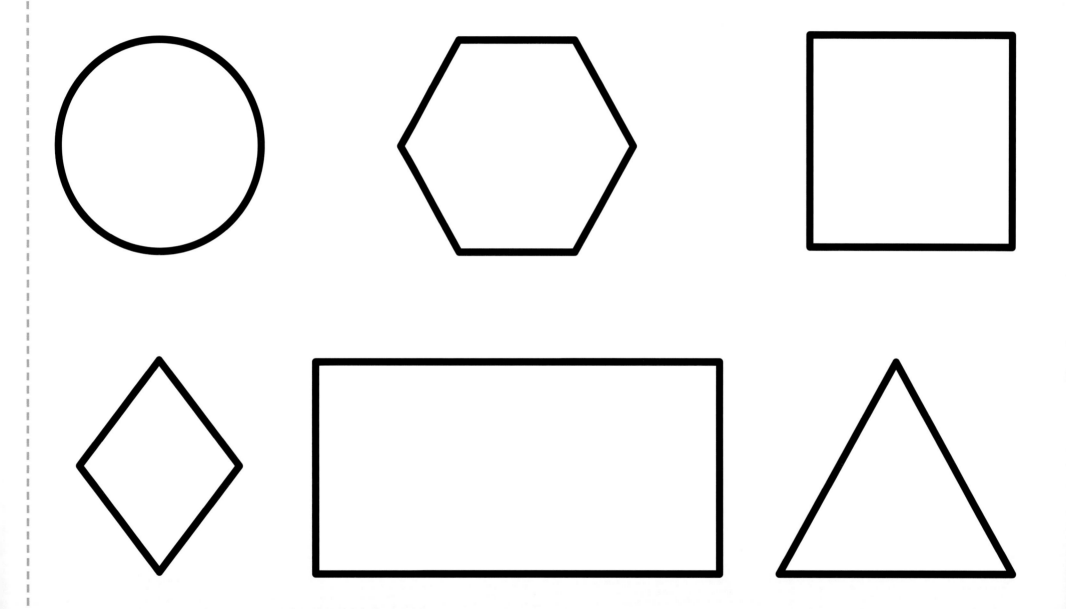

LOOK AND PRINT. HOW DIFFERENT ARE OUR FINGERPRINTS?

LEFT HAND

RIGHT HAND

LOOK AND STICK.

HEAR   TASTE   TOUCH

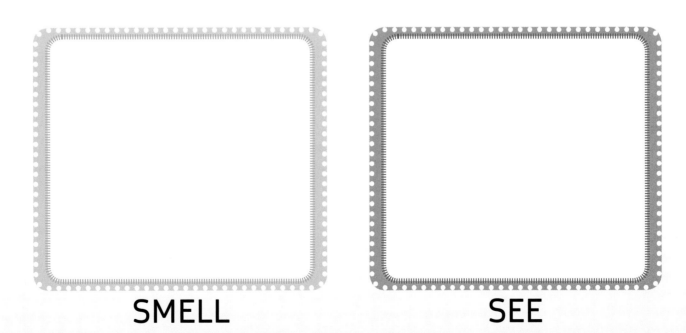

SMELL   SEE

LOOK, LISTEN, AND CIRCLE. WHAT CAN YOU TASTE? WHAT CAN YOU SMELL?

IDENTIFY THE FAMILY MEMBERS.

MOM

DAD

GRANDPA

BROTHER

SISTER

BUILD YOUR FAMILY TREE.

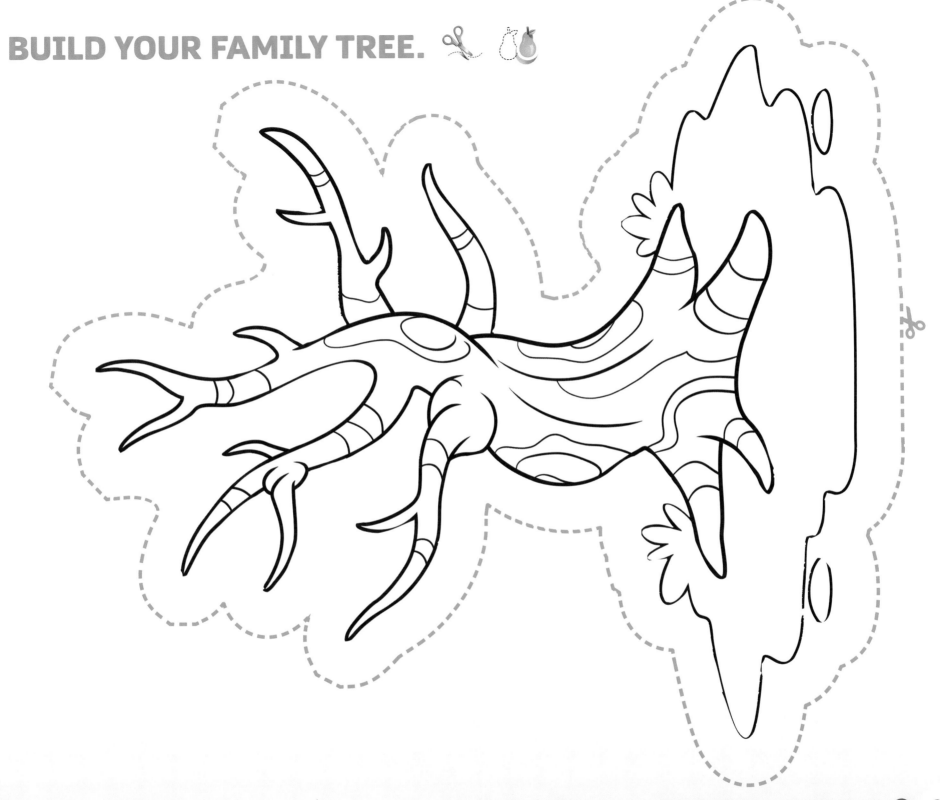

CIRCLE WHAT YOU CAN DO BY YOURSELF. CATEGORIZE, CUT, AND GLUE.

COOK

MAKE THE BED

PLAY

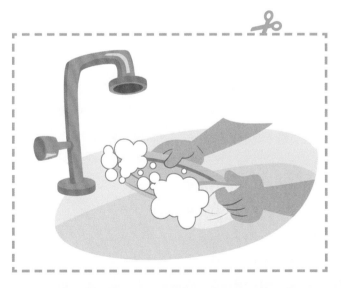

WASH THE DISHES

FEED THE PETS

BUY THINGS

ORDER THE ACTIVITIES.
MAKE AN ACTIVITY CLOCK.

LOOK, CHOOSE, AND MATCH.

COLOR THE ANIMALS THAT LIVE BOTH ON THE LAND AND IN THE SEA.

WHAT HAPPENED TO THE WATER IN EXPERIMENT 1?

BEFORE

AFTER

COLOR THE JARS ACCORDING TO EXPERIMENT 2.

HOT WATER

COLD WATER

STICK THE OBJECTS IN THE CORRECT COLUMN.

TRANSPARENT	TRANSLUCENT	OPAQUE

COUNT THE SPLATS ON THE PAINTINGS. COLOR.

WHICH OBJECT WILL LAND FIRST?

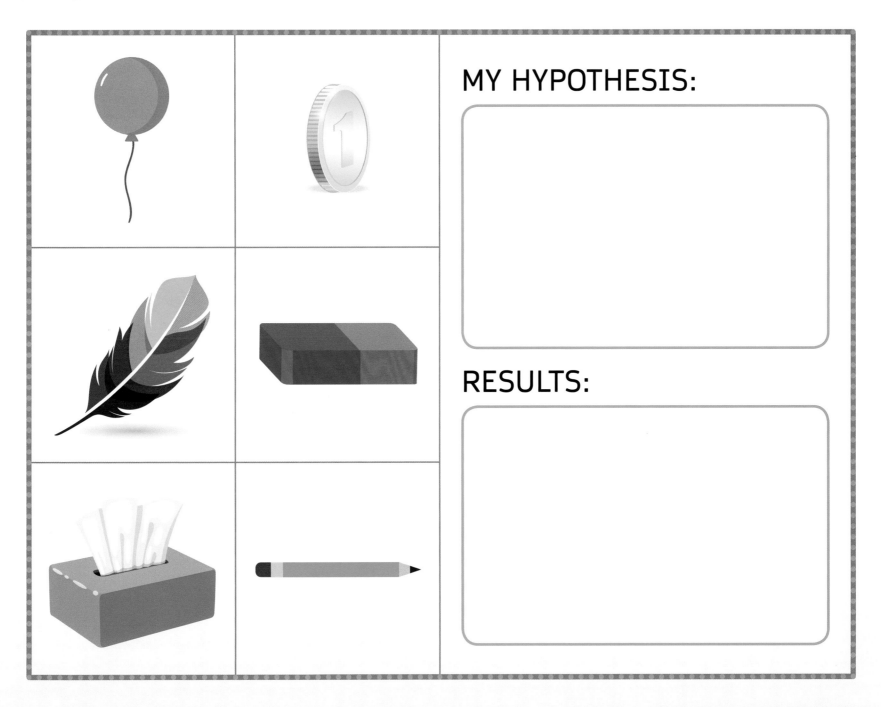

MY HYPOTHESIS:

RESULTS:

LET'S HELP! COLOR. COUNT THE ITEMS WE CAN RECYCLE. 👁 ✏️ ✋3

HOW LONG UNTIL THEY ARE GONE? WRITE.

CIRCLE THE ROOTS YELLOW. CIRCLE THE FLOWERS RED. CIRCLE THE LEAVES BLUE. CIRCLE THE SEEDS GREEN.

COLOR AND STICK THE CHARACTERS IN THE CORRECT ORDER.

DRAW YOUR FOOD MACHINE.

CREATE A DELICIOUS ACROSTIC.

COLOR THE DOMESTIC ANIMALS.

GLUE DOMESTIC ANIMALS IN THE YARD.

MATCH EACH ANIMAL WITH WHAT IT NEEDS.

BUILD A BIRD FEEDER.

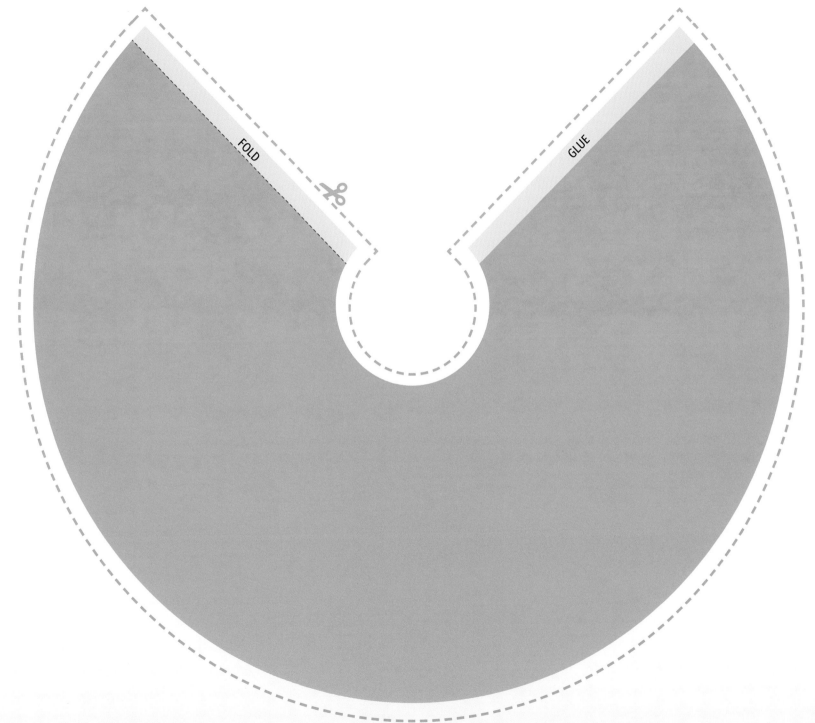

FOLD

GLUE

CIRCLE YOUR FAVORITE PLACE IN TOWN.
THEN CIRCLE YOUR PARENTS' FAVORITE PLACES IN TOWN.

DRAW YOUR FAVORITE PLACE IN TOWN AND GLUE IT.

ADD NUMBERS FROM DICE TO COLOR THE FIRE TRUCK. 3

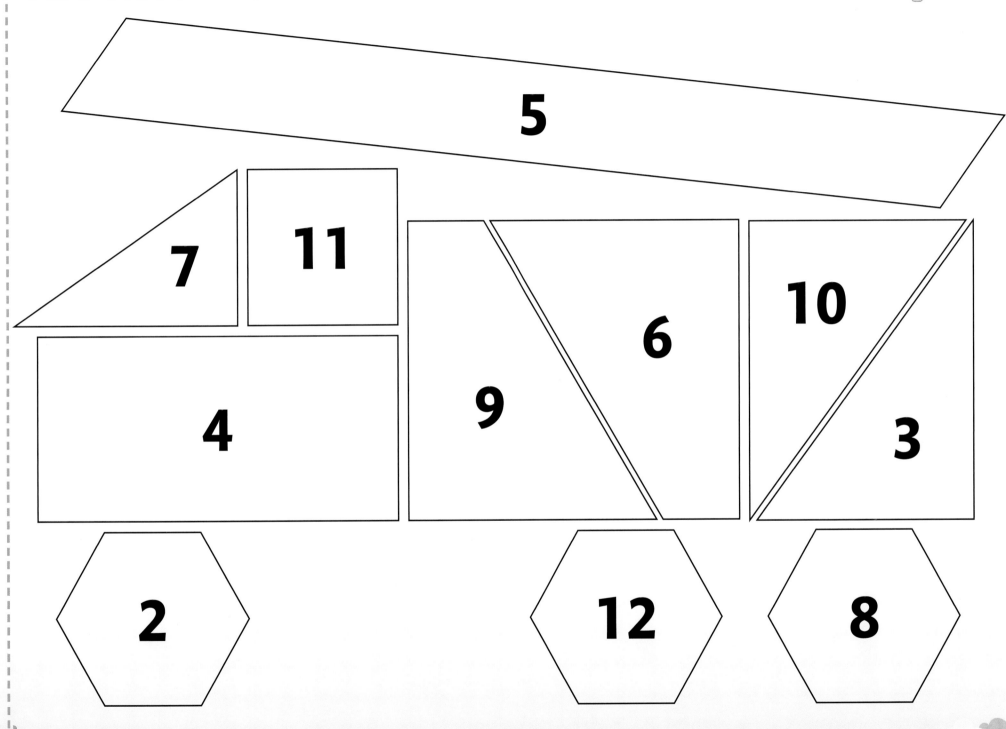

IDENTIFY EACH WORKPLACE. STICK THE PROFESSIONAL WHO WORKS THERE.

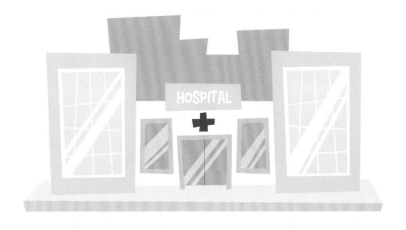

DRAWING

DRAW.

DRAW.

DRAW.

DRAW.

STICKERS

STICKERS

UNIT 2

UNIT 4

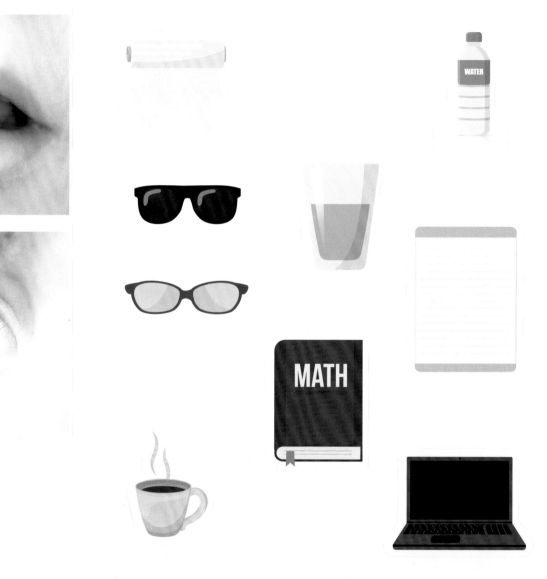

STICKERS

UNIT 6

UNIT 8